# GANGSON

# GANGSON

**Andy Weaver**

NeWest Press

# 2011

**Library and Archives Canada Cataloguing in Publication**

Weaver, Andy, 1971–

Gangson / Andy Weaver.

Poems.

ISBN 978-1-897126-72-1

I. Title.

PS8595.E175G36 2011     C811'.6     C2010-906766-5


Editor: Douglas Barbour
Cover and interior design: Natalie Olsen, Kisscut Design
Author photo: Kelly Laycock

NeWest Press acknowledges the support of the Canada Council
for the Arts, the Alberta Foundation for the Arts, and the Edmon-
ton Arts Council for our publishing program. We acknowledge the
financial support of the Government of Canada through the Canada
Book Fund for our publishing activities.

#201, 8540–109 Street Edmonton, Alberta T6G 1E6
NeWest Press 780.432.9427   www.newestpress.com

*No bison were harmed in the making of this book.*
printed and bound in Canada    1  2  3  4  5  13  12  11  10

# CONTENTS

## Caledonian Poison

reversed or nothing uncanny, your allusion is of free humour to a stranger. in your marriage I become pock-pudden. the same lame man devoured all my halts; he served his sister, and the upstrained bury-case was home again. The bee's very body was a muchly supper, politic for never, and, midst breakfast, made a homily of your marriage's next ill. He himself knows mourning; this proves him a man more agile than others. was your inferiority somehow a promise, an abiding, fleshly obedience to my horn, my kin, my blood? when the iron called, the wiser had romantic names for trans-national means and ends. his tale of hell was Jonah's alone. the punishment of husbandry. use and question were swallowed by her mighty Ireland (he took the belly case before it was sure to soothe her whaling union). I own comical accord. history is a shallow bull of papish pamphlets — the dissolution treated marriage like a union betwixt former poor capacities of drudge; all circumstances become subjected whether you tend the barns equally or with a new constitution. Hose and take up the name, vindicate the scots bull with the bottom of your glass.

## Grandfather Coelacanth

inscrutable thingness
time's syncopation

air swelling your body like a soporific
like words trapped in the tongue

bearer of sopheric knowledge
first witness of solar flare

lost to science as the search
for the material nature of love

altar of ribs
primitive cathedral of air

found as lovers often are
gnawing at the bend of a hook

scientists so carefully cut
to sound the beating of your heart

word
before language

madding eye
in skeletal head

## The loon's red eye

conductor
of an older current


a golden chalice held


judgment
of guilt

## The Cacophony
(Cribsong of Corvus corax)

         corpuscular corpus     delecti
      countermanded countries of creation


counterfeit
    counterphobic
counterpoise
    counterattack
counter     culture


      cousin coyote cozens the cowslips
      crocuses cower near the creak
      coves of crabbed coral
      criminate crowds of crucifers


        courtesans    of the cowcatcher
        crackdown    on the cretins
        crow    for crackbrained creatures


        cull    cuckolds    from the cumulus

a couvade countermeasure

a covenanter curtsies courtly love

maven craven couturier

courses across the coverlet


can't curfew this curate's egg


A COSEISMAL COSMOGRAPHY

A COUP DE GRACE

A COUP D'ETAT

A COUP DE THEATRE


**us ravens / ravenous**


can't correct our corruption

'cause we

corrupt

cant

## Children + clumsiness = disaster

(a found poem)

*For Monica Flegel*


Jack + Jill
incline 1 in 8
puff pant summit +
pail Bubble-bubble-splash
incline 20° + carelessness =
biff bump rattle SPLOSH
Jack minus water plus
crown + abrasion of
epidermis + Jill
weight 4 stone
2 lb. =
Misery.

**man     the civil     and behalf**

                                       truth
of   is he truth     truthful
telling story   banking     disclosure made
a toady by   controversial computer
function   path   configurations are oracular
used abacus trying   tried he
to theatre   to ablebodied   to
tobacco patience   open in italianate
something often   and make something
to try   there succeeding   put-on test see
to see   aptitude it   use
the toboggan   someone   job blubber
out to in   place in
play a made ball   entitling
attempt   into causing worry   nutlike
the epicarp   the hole governor
carolina against atheist   as he
causes   attempt given   succinct

**6:43am Eastern Standard Time but 4am Atlantic Standard Time Wednesday, February 10, 2010**

start at the stopping
a trick
of perspective

passing
what

stop

glottal st

op

anthropology
that breaks

brea
kdo
wn

bray

O Whystan, tell me again
of the suffering masters

each clutches at
his grief like a rare coin

I dream of the solace of good forms

Bray, stupid ass, bray
I will expiate my pettiness
pettily

the liminal beloved
of philosophers and
Romantic poets. Space
between the dictionary entries

Rehearsals and recitations
petty recreations and
could you please turn up
that country song?

Swallow words and bring them
back up again, chew my cud
and stare blank
black eyes

This is stupid stuff,
best left
to Victorians or, better yet,
Georgian hacks.

But at my back I always hear
Hawking's mechanical drone
tallying the stars. Easier, really,
to count the one black space.

That there will be no easy epiphanies
is itself the easiest epiphany.

*not that the words are heavy*
*but that we are so weak*

no place left but the wooden fire
escape. like it is a bird-boned shoulder
in my hands.

like it. like

it it.

like

its it
it
like

*"Much worse is the loss of that person's past, of his or her*
*memory and thus of his or her experience; death, as far as we*
*can tell, obliterates the emotional intellect in which enormous*
*intensities of response radiate and in which the fabric of the*
*significance of everything that has been woven into it exists."*

a rest
arrest
this rest
dross
dross

dross

## The usual lines

backward glances and glances to the side,
a mixture of sun and clouds, soft turbulence
at the right or wrong elevations.

(there was no vote (in the great democracies
in the countries (we call another world


in a world of grand gestures,
how the ants hug the baseboard
as they move through my house. the uselessness
of the daily necessities.


making an X last night with silver cutlery at the end of the
meal washed down with several bottles of good riesling while
we giggled over the desert tray)))

birds pushed from the nest too soon believe they are flying.

i've organized my books through a belief in the alphabet.

the summit, mountaineers say, is only halfway.


*Tuesday, September 11, 2007*

## BBC World News

blood around the badger's mouth reminds me of Hawthorne's
courage. in the face of such, yawning is impossible.
this loan word will put you between a brook and a rock.
Clare enjoys his close shave, like the rest of us.

do you have the eggshells in your boots? i hear the
wind in the willows and the dogs won't save you now.
"We can categorically state that we have not released
man-eating badgers into the area."

## gone starling

spring singers
bringers of songs
springsteen's third encore
at the steeltown arena

a polyphony of one
placeholder for gulls
shakespeare's best
gift to the new world

rudderless hurlers of flight
sexy teachers of grammar
in bad pantsuits
fire the young man's
glans ritual
late-night lodestar lingamism

first fans of john cage
preparers of nature's piano
reclaimers of every ledge
in the name of high school smokers

slang rit glint ars poetica

pretenders to the proclaimers throne
soap box vox
vox populi vox dei
redd foxx vox
swamp fox with a feather
in your cat nobody knows
where the squawk box is at

carpetbagger as interpreted by beckett
waiting for nothing, waiting to go

all-star linguists
gnarl its latin grs

scat man as the scat splats
full grown midgets of tweet tweet
tweet sockin rockin robins

slant rig rang silt
from an art sling
tan girls
doing shots

with a salt grin
while all the phones in the world
call their last ring

machine of sound coming apart at the seems
keeping it all together for one more meme
morphemes so keen even morphine bleeds spleen

wheezer tweezing notes from empire of song
squeeze box song, folk song,
how could something so wrong be so sleight
who knew that street meat could taste so sweet
baby, you ever hear of a big sportscar,
i'll make you a star, make you see stars,
show you the on-star link to paradise,
once you go starling you're everybody's darling

no?
then fuck you, cowbird, and the gorse you floated in on

**lyric poetry**

there comes a time
in every man's life
when he no longer
expects to hear hall
& oates playing in
a public place but
once he learns to
accept that inevitability maneater!

## They both cover the letting of blood

what if michael jackson really was
bad? whose to blame
for this mess? dude, where's
my caravaggio? how's that
carbon-based life form
treating you? where's your parade?
what the hell? what the fuck? did anyone
ever find that beef? are you talking
to me? will you still respect me
when the poem's over? where *have*
all the flowers gone? when can I
go into the whorehouse and buy
what I need with my good looks? how's
that objective correlative treating you?
who do you think you are? when
wasn't our concept of historical past
a simulacrum? How is a ballot like a scab?

is that my old friend, angst? what
happened to our dependence
on domestic wheelbarrows? when did
we lose our attention to etail? I'm a lazy man
— isn't bisexuality a lot of work?
who do I think you are? how's that fifth
sense treating you? where do you think I am?
hey, how's that winnable war going? when
did he become cliche guevara? who gets
out of here alive? who screams
for ice cream?

## Class Order

(for Adam Dickinson)

Abstract ideas
      abstractly
           in a concrete manner

Ethics is not   the reward
The reward   is the reward

           Each word a shovel
      The only way to dig
is down

        Each hole wholly present
        in a holy past

           A precision not careless
              of the abundance

Attention to the old rituals:
    the auguries of weather
    the fat agony of squirrels
    in a delayed winter
    a grandfather's watch

Ah, when you consider
    the radiance

Attention is to coin
the realm

## a ghazal for d.b.

dug that jazz, a red shift,
saskatchewan nights when nihilism is the easy choice

cage brings his beneficence
and brings out an urge to bow

no one knows why the mushrooms grow
in their arcing paths, notes written without a staff

a web hums naked resonance,
silently, the voice will fill us

the language growing on without us
starlings and whales left to pick up the slack

o teacher, what is that sound, like a violin in the hands
of a marble cutter, one without the deft touch of a barber?

## 273 Seconds from John Cage

(To Whom It Did Concern)


                    cracking Sound
                         davId tudor breathes
                    as he Lifts a
                         kEyboard lid
                         oNe two three
                times all while Composing
                    himsElf

## GANGSON

*Possible*
*To use*
*Words provided one treat them*
*As enemies.*
*Not enemies — Ghosts*
*Which have run mad*
*In the subways*
*And of course the institutions*
*And the banks. If one captures them*
*One by one proceeding*

*Carefully they will restore*
*I hope to meaning*
*And to sense.*

George Oppen, "A Language of New York"


*I too question the audacity of a structure that explains everything.*

Lisa Robertson, *XEclogue*


*It is States that make wars and not nations.... We cannot crusade*
*against war without crusading against the State.*

Randolph Bourne, "The State"

Those who cannot remember the condemned repeat the past

## 1. The cradle

first     of terrorized New York     a frequent
town and present     theatrical district

a howling wilderness     in which the savage
expeditions     penetrated wilderness

accounts of riot     in
time of gangs and underworld     nothing with outbreaks

venturesome journeys     to settlements     in Harlem
drain the area and     throw it open     to settlement

a canal from pond to Hudson but     dug so
later     when the earth had sufficiently

been laid out     extended site     of
merchants     Broadway and City Hall     and

revel     in the gardens     of the commoners flock
the means of artificial     dancing was free

the customer     bought an occasional glass     of ale porter or
custom     for a hero with a loathing     send his

young and   handsome wife into the street   each night   carrying
Whitechapel              districts of London

the Ward comprised     eighty-six
pieces of glass   and colored paper

some taste    for decoration     and seamen
every obscure grave    giving up its dead

dogs howl to lie   men women and boys slink              off
the fear    that you have     to rescue

crazy loved dens of death   down headlong      down filthy
wide on the southern     of irregular width

prints show  three stories       but      writers say
there were five

## 2. Early Points

original genesis      the tenement
murderers     and Forty Thieves

the first    New York     a
enormous plug hat        stuffed with wool and leather

ears      as helmets
In the slang      rabbit rowdy     and a dead rabbit very

gradually     declined     amusement center
weathering many storms      theatre renamed

still    the shadows    of the avenue railroad
filled       with respectable

families     drank pink   and yellow
degradation     the gallery     of theater

a few years       the erection
brasses and dices       and sometimes rifles for

Everything was free       except
interest      shoot the

common    joined fights    with roaring
screech battle    rushed biting and    clawing

midst of a mass most    stouthearted
metropolis    formation

a paid fighting force    of great event
pantaloons full    as the modern Oxford

heavy boots    on the back    of his head
grave    immortalized    by writing

The Bowery    performed clamorous
a car off    the tracks    a few blocks on

shoulders uproariously    bumping passengers
the barrel For dessert    and very fond

the cherry tree
gained enormous following    of voters

Native Americans    took the place    of the Whigs
an Englishman named    the police    the rioters

from the playhouse    they roared    down Rose street
stripped    and parcelled among    the gangsters shame

A few blocks of story    origin    the name colonial
trysting place    the townspeople    called From

houses and stores    on fire
barrels of flour    and a thousand    bushels of wheat

a large body    of police supported by
powerful control of the absolute

frequently appealed to    the police to    quell riots
The excitement was    intense

a great crowd    stood in front
and never    returned    his country

## 3. along the front

before the Revolution    for years thereafter
inaugurated President Hancock

who conceived the present plan    of America
inspiration    for the Sunshine of Paradise

a little side street    such as often
street over cobble stones    rolled the carriages

aristocrats    filled    with sheltered members
haunted place    other

a snatch    a member    of the Slaughterhouse
corner of Dover    run by One Armed

trusted lieutenants    all and Gall
push him    to infuriated Slobbery

promptly seized    the prominent nose
to the Point    on important forays

Sailors frequented    as they slept
at the Glass    for more than a year

prison    for life    he killed
harlots bartenders and musicians    at noon

expounded a passage from the Scriptures
meetings whenever    drunk enough to give her

consent and    at length    they prevailed upon to abandon
Cherry    resort gin mill in Water

overrun by preachers
services the public need    be deceived in the matter

of his reformation    His motive
clubbed    A fellow they had never seen

I must be damned    good looking    to have so many fine fellows
declare it was all    a put up job

## 4. River rat

gangsters pointy
more     a match for the Dead

Rabbit        Plug Ugly
considerably enlarged    field of operation

excellent qualities   with the Roger    flying
abject surrender   of rival   dipped into

trophies returned    one female ear   to its owner
his junior    most celebrated

the member   the many noted
Johnson heavy   as always   great events

portend a man   of small   courage  he
shook hands with

Slobbery Jim
shipping in

an exhaustive study
base opportunities

along the dock
a night imbibed too

deeply          sought
evasive answers          obtained

ol Wild Bill
more or less    quiescent

## 5. The Killing Butcher

His   larger business in
spread      and gold   costly ware

exquisite cut   an embrace
commonly held        the champion eye

gouger of time   ferocious expert
he boasted

his       ballot boxes   honest
his rightful place       among the powers

lynched the
gentlemen

seized the nape of the neck    and dragged
miles   to sport

One night a week      the hands
seized two huge carving knives        inviting choice

## 6. The Dead Rabbit

common remainder     of the country
the current theater     trained their heaviest guns

had the town by the ears
public cause     for eager salaries

fortunes in real estate     secured the names
indignant     demanded and procured release

successful thrusts
this advent     swarmed

## 7. The Draft

The fighting     of the New
United slums .   mob is not people     nor

belong to people     made of
circumstance     craving plunder     a barbarous spite

a different race     a disposition to bolster     the failing
individual     swarmed     the streets

        frenzied men     and women
whom some     of the fights

were outnumbered     at least     to one but
appeared the balcony of residence     and addressed a large

        pastoral letter entitled
men armed with iron     visit a new

Liberty     for aid and
retain     the routine     for the day

hot and clear     the sun was not ours
the mass     surged   the street moved

columns        along avenues brandishing
    grown proportions     while the Marshal

drew    the spinning wheel     of paper
building        firemen     compelled to stand

destruction of the entire
other        mauled toward

a huge thug    with a club
thirteen commands        attack

avenue    and street     outnumbered
being        rescued     and defeated    in turn

losses                the vast mass     surging        tumultuous
    instant        was checked and    attacked

ferocity Before troops could reload        their
terrific blows            tremble

## 8. Riots continue

day began
        skull     a stone weighing

dropped time
a demonstration

windows and doors    bricks and paving stones
street      deployed its men

skirmishers    police   slowward
wheel in company

volleys        with fury
flesh   with knives

body with       howls
evident      intention

in flames   in rapid fires
thieves in sight    of the shop they had stolen

## 9. When was wicked

frequent     pilgrimages to
a small New    to seek fortune

fallen ways of        most expensive     bordellos
Woods in street     near Broadway

from avenues    the original     Tenderloin
to compete      with such celibate

street      Pastors in street   was
bludgeon for the quickness     seized obstreperous

women by hair      flung them to
Satans Circus

the market   occupied
ladies   twenty cents    but men paid the price

two for a quarter Next door
doggerel inviting    fare to partake

Punches and juleps cobblers and smashes make the tongue wag with
                                  wits merry flashes
girls brought up    from the basement

customs spent       in sorry debauch
served       over a long behind

long dirk and bludgeon were frequent     silence
haunt the Bowery     of thieves pickpockets procurers

## 10. King of the Banks

always demand     of most brilliant sneak
moments          sneaked out     bear

cash and securities     negotiable
house to house    criminals dealt

a bank of distinction     aristocrat
posed     as the wealthy widow

engineer elaborate     functions and furore
unable to save               the reform element

power and procured     indictments
wealth and position     possessed great attitude

everyone suspicious and forbidding
the merchant          had arrived

top speed     to the lawyers home
professional criminals     compel

account of movement    the night was stolen
an offer to deliver     the corpse on conditions

The amount    paid to the Judge
men    clambered and approached

masked and carried    a heavy sack
a cluster of bells    alarm    through the village

## 11. The Whys and times

The tang    of existence
ring the summer

always lunging    in churchyard
efficient beverage    embalming fluid

the Morgue
game    widely known

the Tomb within
a burglar    a sneak    thief

fingers    prying into pockets
a few heads and many windows broken

## 12. Kingdoms of gangs

factions
endorsed          the candidacy          of elected

majority          over George
a story           related with relish

judge who          wished to curry
dollars      to dollars

house to the inmates
to property and large          accounts

Dust      controlled Manhattan
streets

## 13. Prince of Gangsters

moving pictures     stage a way
grace in the glory     of a dress In the days of

Dead Rabbits   and Boys    Dandy
for the purposes

offered   sale
came       to assume the name

sank   his natural social level
enough       to claim sovereignty

artillery     joyfully firing indiscriminate
employ to advantage   rig a hot campaign

hours later
bet his teeth and hand     his revolver at a table

ways and means
hired to protect     he sowed   his wild

dead days
flower and chivalry     assembled nightly revel

Razor   to the resort
he recovered   his wounds

## 14. He Wars

a crooked little thoroughfare
      a careless sign

omitted
New York

slender capital
fumes        smoke

float to the streets
voted them early

often    beloved of
grace   inspired

a gambler    a race of gamblers
celebrated pursuit

Sing of peace
a Sing Sing     policy game

men murdered      the Blood
a calligrapher

ingenious     in the arrangements
With these utensils    beholden to no man

## 15. The Last Wars

the lump          a sudden end
a favorite haunt

Ticker
blazed and collapsed

sweetheart
of exceptional balance

Record    listen          gently
an independent venture    the Blood

tainted
the hates quoted

territory
idly moving

this period      the Haymarket
enhanced its great      natural beauty

the addition of Italian gardens          an art gallery
men armed          with hatchets and crow bars

## 16. The Passing

that name
a cabaret

fancy
over a bottle

whiskey
congregated

Hell
wants      me and you

appointment made      for midnight
In plain language

# WEAVINGS

*I could get here, but I could not get there.*

— *rob mclennan*

1.

laurasia gondwana swirl great panthalassa navel

of the earth tied to the swiveling polaris rock is

alive feel rock's breath in air in your lungs crust

of the earth sloughed skin of the tidal core how

do you stand still ariadnes string tied to the left

horn of the minotaur

2.

one arm of magellan charting the sea the eye the

hurricane spiral through the nebulae murmurs

this mapping is every where meaning my body

all about her body all one piece of string weaved

right is a net

3.

soft steel edge on the unharmed iris temple


throb of living the age of gold razorblades


bite through more than the bracelets of life

4.


shoreline pulse of life abjected from sea and air


and see the crab scuttling sideways along the skin


of two lifes land breaking ocean breaking land salt


water in our lungs the fish a dying cell in the air


water falling off the ospreys wing

5.

Drawing words from your mouth the blister of

memory in the mind bees braille in the petals cup

trace the white outline of hand on the cave wall

drawing your words on the page the

Babelization

6.

flicker cars flicker cars past balcony panels cars in

the flicker periphcry become butterflies butterflies

butterflies in the periphery are butterflies

butterflies lick slick flicker

7.

good fences make good borders this is not about

herons wan goosed uck i can cross a border but

this is redwinge D bird black i can cross a border

but not dodge a cattail looking into the wind

8.

not hell but it'll do jellyfish universe of words a

jagged fingernail across the day's cheek trying to

catch these sounds with your hands only zozer and

imhotep left to change the world

9.

Souljoy trill of reddishgrey leaping from dream to

tree tree to dream bombed silly on cedar rum cat's

ideal of bird dropping berries to the ground like

red wax on a lover's chest on the coldest day of

the year fruit of the alien honeysuckle passing

berries back and forth sentinels in courtship

display sallying like a flycatcher gleaning insects

from leaves undertail coverts fruitbearing

ornaments rustling treeleaves in winters dead

10. Politics

**Queen-Anne's-Lace**-----part of our Peach Rose

Corsage (29.99) @ FTD Florists

**plums** (organic)---2.43/lb

**flowerpot (empty)**----14.99 @ Canadian Tire

**cat**----69.99 @ SPCA (includes free spay or

neuter)

**bull (milkless)**---1734US for an average

Culpepper senior bull @ the Virginia Central Bull

Text Station

**Olympian commentary**---free

**greeny flower asphodel** (useful in menstrual

obstructions and as an antispasmodic)------2.44/lb

@ Health For Everyone Herbs

**Radio Flyer toy red wheel-barrow** (This

wheelbarrow is just like the ones adults use, but

sized for 2 to 5 year olds.. Watch their self-esteem

and self-confidence grow as they really contribute

to outdoor chores by hauling their own load in

their own wheelbarrow! This toy is durable and

will be around long after my children have

outgrown it. "We couldn't be happier with this

purchase of a quality Radio Flyer product", Louise

Carter, New Jersey)---22.49 @ worldwide-

americas.com

**chicken** (free range)---$35.00

Total 1911.33

April 25, 2004.  Much depends upon our attention

to retail.

11.

a ringing in the ears since the paris commune

tells the bureaucracy their week is bloody red

and o so white and we're blue all over

the communards wall in the bright sunshine

heavy with love theres never a blanquist

when you need the name is France

Mr Bond Anatole France

# A Sweet Suite

(4kl)

**Every day**

a world of small

motions

turning on

water

judging time

to test
heat

quick waves
of the hand

the bed sighs
the smell of your hair

eyelash drops
to the ground

just there

spider web in
doorway and

again

the rippling
of tapwater

## Applestar

Not the mcintosh, the red and yellow delicious, but the Granny Smith, a cool green and your eyes so green, my own face reflecting back to me with orbed clarity. My hand softly on your belly.

The mysteries of apple, the smooth polish of its skin, a delicate marble, a universe within as white as ours is black. A stem to show that life begins and slowly ends and that there can be glory in between, the dyingtime called living. It perches in your hand just as a sparrow would not.

A small bite and then the tongue on the fleshy moistness. The simplest equation. Then you cut it just right. You know how to hold everything just so on the steel tip, the knife dawning the apple's white night and, at the centre, a star, an applestar at the beginning, and your navel, and your eyes, and my face reflected.

## Re: Workings

eyes only      to see
you to know    how    to reach
you even if i do    not know
how this    happens
in my    nervous    machine


heart    the red grey    machine only
to beat · a few buckets of water    tied up
in this complicated fig-leaf


hands    and feet only to    move
our mobile    bodies
things    among things    flesh
of flesh

**Theory**

Theory on
the radical
importance of
spatial geography
to the meta/
physical act
of love

```
ill                      ill
  lovey               lovey
      ou          ou
       wit   wit
        H
       in          in
      fin          fin
  ites              ites
pace                  pace
ill                    ill
  lovey             lovey
      ou          ou
       wit   wit
        H
       in    in
      fin          fin
  ite s                  ites
  pac e                      pac    e
      i  l  l                  i        l        l
       l   o    v     e      y              l      o     v    e  y
            o      u                          o          u
            w       i        t              w      i      t
                        H                          H
                 i              n                      i    n
              f  i n                            f     in
               i     t     es                 i     t  es
                p ace                         pace
                     ill      ill
                     lovey  lovey
                     ou        ou
                     wit       wit
                               H
                       in    in
                      fin      fin
                      i  t es    ites
                     p ac e       p ac e
            i      l      l          i    l l
             l  o  v  e    y       l     o   v   e   y
               o u              o    u
              wit         w  i    t
                 H
               in        i n
              fin      fin
          ites      ites
          pace        pace
        ill          ill
      lovey          lovey
      ou          ou
       wit   wit
        H
       in    in
      fin          fin
  ites                  ites
pace                  pace
```

## Homage to Sex at 31

1.

Sailors, of winds; a plowman, concerning his oxen;
Soldiers, the enumeration of wounds; the shepherd, of ewes.


a black fire burning in a fire of white...


the Babel of your body


under my tongue


bocal
               papilla
          pezon
                      mamelon


     dim words
   of a radiant time


Each man where he can, wearing out the night in his manner.


And the rest
       is just

2.

fixed stars and wandering planets
plot the harsh acts of your refusals
Many and many.


As if love, within its
boundaries, is another moon.


3.

lips sounding
the tip
of the buried bell


4.

My mouth is a cup
holding water
from a difficult river.


Black horses drive the sun.
Fish swim in a dry stream.


I serve my term of madness.


5.

O Basho,
the rippling moon
pays us no mind

**I do not understand.**

Higher mathematics,
the point of shopping lists,
the intemperate language
of hungry cats. Anything
past the fifth pint. The tidal
systems, the moon, the twenty
eight-day calendar of blood.
Italian automobiles
or their owners, how eugenics
breeds a better dog, the patience
of the mourning doves as the sparrows
harrow the feeder, the asphodel,
that greeny flower. How, when I lie
in bed a certain way my whole body
is there in your eyes. I understand I do
not understand.

**you and i**
(4kl)

you
were the robin and i was the worm and i was the song and
you were Cohen and you were the weeping birch and i was
the newly rediscovered ivory billed woodpecker and i was
the wind and you were the spider dangling from the leaf
and you were the bookworm and i was the parchment and

i

was the goose quill and you were the india ink and you were
david inspired by the lord and i was the trembling reed and i
was the apple and you were the tongue-licked lips and you
were the fever and i was the infection and i was the needle
and      you      were      the      bending      skin      and

you

were the paratactical movement and i was the *and* sitting
bloodied in the doorway and i was the gazelle and you were
the cheetah's unretractable claws and you were the windmill
and i was the wheat and i was glistening and you were the
beaded sweat and you were the napalm and i was the order
and

i

was chaos and you were the theory and you were the cry of
fire and i was the crowded theatre and i was the tv and you
were the batteries in the remote and you were the hymen and
i was awkward frustration and i was my teenage burgeon-
ing desire and you were smiling with staples in your belly
and

you

were Yankee carpetbaggers and i was gone with the wind
and i was General Lee and you were Bo Duke's blond ass
sliding over the hood and you were Loverboy and i was
Reno's red leather pants and i was the elegy and you were
the churchyard and you were St. Elizabeth's and i was usury
and

i

was Freud and you were envious of something and you
were Freud and i was as peripheral as Oedipus's stepdad
and i put the lack in Lacan and you were the baby look-
ing back in the mirror and you were David Antin and i
was Robert Kroetsch and i was Robert Duncan and you
were John Crowe Ransom and that's going too far and

you

were sweet red wine and i was the cup overrunneth and
i was the window and you were the shaft of light and you
were the batsignal and i was the convenient full moon on
the night of the crime and i was the trapdoor and you were
the rope and you were the hand slapping leather and i was
the                    bullet                    and

i

was the compliment and you were something weren't you
and you put the tit in antitemporality and i was sure glad
and i put the razz in the razzamatazz and you were the
bopping beat and you were the ragtime piano and i was
joplin's jangling fingers and i was the cool cat scatting and
you        were        clambering        jeoffry        and

you were the delicate blue eggshell and i was the robin

## Notes

The poems in this book constantly allude to, borrow from, and were inspired by the writings and ideas of others. While I note some of the less obvious borrowings below, this list is by no means complete, often owing to my habit of writing down exciting ideas or lines and then forgetting who wrote them.

"6:43am Eastern Standard Time but 4am Atlantic Standard Time Wednesday, February 10, 2010" borrows the italicized prose quotation from Lyn Hejinian's "Comments for Manuel Brito."

"BBC World News" was inspired by (and borrows the last line from) a 2007 report by the BBC about the possibility that British forces had released man-eating badgers around one of their bases in Iraq.

"273 Seconds from John Cage" was inspired by Cage's *4'33"* and follows his rules for mesostics.

"Gangson" is an examination of New York's distant and not-so-distant history of violence. The poem is a cut-up of Herbert Asbury's 1927 book, *The Gangs of New York*. I took the first and last line of each page and typed them out as a series of couplets. The first poem contains the couplets from the first chapter (following the book's order), the second poem contains those couplets from the second chapter, etc. Once the couplets were compiled, I removed words until each couplet started to make its own sense. In some instances, due to short lines or lines consisting only of names or something equally uninteresting to me, I expanded the couplet to include the line directly after the top or directly before the bottom of the page. Many of the couplets were removed completely as I whittled the poem down to its current state.

I had no specific, preconceived message to convey; I was interested in the themes of violence and corruption that presented themselves to me from Asbury's text. However, in my mind, at least, these themes are relevant to the current political situation, given New York City's position as the imaginary ground zero of hostilities in the so-called War on Terror.

"Weavings" is an attempt to tie together disparate elements of my reading and thinking at specific times. Rather than a stream of consciousness (which reaffirms the individual as monad) these pieces are intended as a tapestry constructed from the work, words, and ideas of many others.

"Homage to Sex at 31" was written after rob mclennan requested poems in response to Barry McKinnon's "Sex at" poems. The poem was inspired by McKinnon's work and Ezra Pound's "Homage to Sextus Propertius."

## Acknowledgements

Some of the poems in this book have appeared (occasionally in markedly different versions) in the following publications: *CV2, The Fiddlehead, filling Station, Pottersfield Portfolio, The Olive, PRECIPICe, Qwerty, Spire Poetry Poster*, and *The Windsor Review*. "Caledonian Poison" and "Children + clumsiness = disaster" appeared in the chapbook *Disaster!* (one trick pony, 2004). "The Cacophony" was commissioned by the *Edmonton Journal*. rob mclennan published early drafts of the first few sections of "gangson" in the online journal *Ottawater*; *West Coast Line* also published a large selection of later sections.

My sincerest thanks to the editors of each of these publications. As far as I'm concerned, your amps all go to 11.

I would also like to thank the Alberta Foundation for the Arts, who provided a grant that allowed me time to work on this collection at a formative stage.

I owe a great debt to Adam Dickinson, Steve McOrmond, and Matthew Tierney, who each provided invaluable suggestions and support as I worked to finish this collection.

"6:43am Eastern Standard Time but 4am Atlantic Standard Time Wednesday, February 10, 2010" is for my Nana, Dorothy Gilks (1915-2010), much adored by all who knew her.

This book is for Kelly Laycock; may you continue to do that voodoo that you do so well.

**Andy Weaver** lives near Toronto, and he teaches poetry and poetics at York University. His first book, *Were the Bees,* also published by NeWest Press, was a finalist for the 2006 Stephan G. Stephansson Award for Poetry.